IT'S ALL ABOUT YOU

INSPIRATIONS
TO LIVE YOUR
BEST LIFE YET

LATHAM C. ALEXANDER, JR.

In Loving Memory
of Margaret Glenn
a.k.a. Big Ma

CONTENTS

FOREWORD

All outcomes are about decisions. We create our destiny the moment we decide, no matter how trivial. Yet, as James Clear, author of *Atomic Habits* proclaims, most often humans organically move toward options that require the least amount of work. In many instances this results in mediocrity. To the contrary, people who rise beyond what they see in the natural are better positioned to practice a growth mindset. This is the zone Latham Alexander invites readers to experience in *It's All About You!*

Life really is all about you. How do I know this for sure? Because I am reminded of life's greatest commandment, *Love God and love others as yourself* (Matthew 22: 37 – 39). To love others as yourself implies that you love yourself. Consequently, the measure of your love for self is equivalent to the extent of love you can extend to others. When you focus on yourself and become the best version of yourself, you can share the best of who are with your neighbor. In a nutshell, loving yourself is a prerequisite to treating others with the highest regard. This life is about you and how you show up to relate with others and the environment.

Research shows the way you view yourself profoundly affects the way you live your life. Perspective is crucial. I always say, "The way you see what you see determines what you see." To realize your fullest potential, you must not concern yourself with the judgment of others, but rather give your attention to improvement. In this way, a true decision leads to achievement because it involves commitment to action. Action is not about instant perfection. It is about confronting challenges and making progress that matter most. This is the mindset of a champion, someone striving for excellence. When you are determined to live your best life, you understand that setbacks are par for the course. Challenges become fuel for motivation and inform subsequent actions.

In *The Happiness Advantage*, Shawn Anchor reminds readers that happiness is about the joy one experiences when operating through their potential. Latham's story reflects expressions of his potential as he strives for the best in himself, for himself, and for his family. This is evident in the decisions he made and continues to make. Anchor might suggest Alexander's success was preceded by happiness. One does not become a success before experiencing a level of happiness. Success then, is a by-product of happiness.

If there is an ounce of truth to this idea, Alexander accurately forecast achievement with the notion of focusing on yourself and the decisions you make as a competitive advantage. When you make life all about you, in essence you make life about others. That is success. That is a win—win.

Dr. Larthenia Howard
2-time award-winning author
How to Write a Best Seller in 31 Days System®

It's All About YOU

MY SUPERPOWER

Superpower –
"ability that makes or helps you to succeed."

I have used self-reflection as a superpower for long as I can remember, so the idea for my first published book came from a need to help myself as much as a desire to help others. I believe everyone can benefit from self-reflection. It is especially helpful if you are not satisfied with where you are or where you are going in life. Over the years, I have come to rely on introspection in making decisions, small and big. The ability to listen to your intuition, that faint whisper inside can serve as a North Star, or navigational tool when you are confident that you know what you are doing and when you have no clue what you should do next. Either way, when you tap into your inner source of guidance, you will receive the counsel you seek. This book invites you to reflect or to look back while moving forward in your best life yet.

Several years ago, I learned something valuable from a brilliant young lady. I will forever remember those words, "*We must learn from what has or has not happened to us in the past.*" Hindsight truly does empower you with foresight—what you need to do or not to do in the future. Those actions produce insight and allow you to create oversight. Without oversight thoughts and behaviors can be costly in every aspect of your being—financially, emotionally, and in relationships. It is this introspection that drives my success and passion to create something marvelous for me and my family.

In pursuit of living your best life yet, comes a risk of falling short of your dreams, or failure to reach your desired outcomes. It is easy to be sidetracked or even sidelined by others who may have a different agenda. But I encourage you to stay the course. Self-preservation is an inescapable law of nature. Who or what is more important than you? Take a moment to ponder your response to the question. If you need more time to think, let me help you. The answer is—no one. I repeat. No one is more important than you. At the risk of sounding narcissistic, selfish, or egotistical, if you do not place yourself at the center of your world and act from the best of intentions in every relational interaction, eventually you fall short of who you were created to be. You have an obligation to concern yourself with matters that directly affect the development and maturation of who you are and who you are becoming because every decision you make depends on this framework.

This book is for you if you have ever been confused about the "what next" in your life decisions. This book is for you if you have ever doubted yourself, your abilities, or questioned who you are. My hope is that this book reaches you especially if you have ever thought *there has got to be more to life than your current experiences.* Reflect on the stories as I give you a peek of some of my most notable experiences and decisions. Consider how you perceive similar situations in your life or how you might act the same or differently. Dig deep as you approach interacting with the activities that culminate each of the chapters. If you are anything like me, you may notice subtle or overt ideas as to how you can behave in different ways while influencing your personal development for the better.

Here's to your best life yet!

Latham

It's All About YOU

IT'S ALL ABOUT YOU!

YOU

"USED TO REFER TO THE PERSON OR PEOPLE
THAT THE SPEAKER IS ADDRESSING"

Why you?

Why not you?

Who better than you?

You have the resources within yourself to figure out what is best for you. As a friend of mine would say, *"Everything is Figureoutable."* There are many questions you can ask that will lead you to an answer, but I want you to consider these four simple words. What do you want? I know you were probably waiting for some profound, hard to understand prophetic nonsense, but this does not need to be convoluted. The answer to that question is a simple solution to many otherwise difficult situations.

At 14 years old, I sat in the window of our 11th floor, two-bedroom low-income apartment on the West side of Chicago. The apartment was located in one of the most dangerous gang infested areas known as Henry Horner projects. After dealing with multiple physical confrontations with my so-called friends, I was looking out over the neighborhood. I recall thinking we should have fallen prey to the dangers and temptations of our environment. Riots and gang wars were commonplace. The Vice Lords, Disciples, Black Souls and Blackstone Rangers were rampant in our neighborhood. All the gangs recruited on a regular basis. Recruitment was simple, gang members would walk up to you and tell you to follow them. You did not ask questions or refuse. Though I was never recruited, I remember it like yesterday. I was walking with three childhood friends across a large open-field playground where we occasionally played football. The playground connected three housing projects. As we walked, we noticed a large group of older boys walking toward us. We did not recognize them but sensed what was about to happen. One of my partners suggested we try to make a run for it. We knew that would not have been cool, so we continued to walk ahead. When the group of Vice Lords reached us, all three of my friends were pointed out and told to follow the group. One of the Vice Lords looked at me and said, "What's happening little brother?" I responded, "You". For some reason they turned and told my buddies to follow them. Our friendship was never the same. My friends turned on me one by one.

Without a doubt, God and the prayers of my mom protected me and my brothers and sisters. I remember raising my head and eyes to the sky, and at that moment tears began to run down my face. As I reflected on what I had already experienced in my incredibly young life, I said to God,

"Lord, I know and believe in my heart there's a better place and a better life out there for me and my family."

At 14 years of age, I honestly believed what I saw and experienced was all there was to life. My daily experiences became my lifelong reality, or at least in my mind during those tender years. And, at the same time, I knew there was better, a better place in this world that existed outside of the projects. I wanted better and dreamed of better. I believed better existed then and I believe it now.

No matter where you are in life, better exists. How do I know this to be true? Because this phrase can be found in an all-time bestselling book:

"The thief comes only to steal and kill and destroy. I came that they may have life and have it abundantly"

John 10:10

We can debate the context of the Scripture; however, I know this for sure—you, we were created in the image of a Creator who desires the absolute best for each of us. He is glorified through you and how you live your life. The best version of you glorifies Him. You were created to experience the good life in abundance. Believe there is more.

It's All About YOU

My mother, Margaret Alexander, was a single parent for some time. She divorced my father, Latham C. Alexander, Sr., when I was two years old. After the divorce, she provided for me, my sister Deleatrice and brother Glen. We are stairsteps in age and it could not have been easy to care for three small children, but she did and did it rather well. My mother gave us what we needed and sometimes what we wanted if she could. Even though we lived in the hood, we were by no means a product of our surroundings. We went to private Catholic schools and attained what can be considered as a good education. My sister received a four-year scholarship to DePaul University of Chicago, and I attended Loyola University of Chicago. My brother completed cosmetology school and I later did the same. It's amazing how my mother was able to send us to private schools. She earned a dental assistant salary but managed to stretch every penny to the fullest. I believe that is where I got my determination and drive.

I learned how to dream by watching my mom. She did not have to tell me to dream big. I learned by watching. It was clear she wanted more for her children than our present circumstances at the time. There was something out there waiting for each of us, and she did everything in her power to be sure we realized that truth.

This is the truth I hope you realize for yourself as well. You can achieve what you set out to do if you believe you can and are equipped with the skill set. It sounds simple and cliche but believing in this notion is critical to every goal you set. You must believe in yourself and your dreams.

In addition to believing in yourself and your goals, you must surround yourself with people who are genuinely rooting for you to succeed. Identify your greatest supporters. I invite you to take out a sheet of paper and note the names of people you know you can count on to support your dreams. Your list may be short, or it may be long, the point is to recognize your support team and be intentional in your apprecia-tion of their energy. Likewise, keep naysayers at arm's length. Be aware of energy zappers and people who almost always have a "*But*" to share.

John Stuart Mill, former member of Parliament of the United Kingdom, wrote "*One person with a belief is equal to a force of 99 who have many interests.*" The power of belief is immeasurable and cannot be over-rated. My mother's belief in me helped carry the force of my goals by 99. But the reality is this, belief in myself was the magic. How you see yourself will determine how you show up in the world. If you see yourself as inconsistent, you will show up inconsistent. If you see yourself as weak or confused, you will show up as weak and confused. If you see yourself as clear and focused, you will show up clear and focused. It is difficult to be or show up as someone you do not believe yourself to be. What matters most is what you believe about yourself. This requires self-management. And only you can manage you and what you honestly believe. From this stance, self-leadership is critical.

John Maxwell, an American author, would say "A leader is one who knows the way, goes the way, and shows the way." Self-leadership is the foundation for you to understand who you are, which qualifies you to lead you—the foremost authority. As we navigate through life our experiences and challenges prepare and develop us into the people we are and the people we are becoming. With those experiences, we become experts to continue to help ourselves and others. This is important because some mistakes are disastrous and especially when made more than once. Wisdom involves learning from our mistakes and those of others. This depth of insight requires intentionality with clarity and focus.

There is a danger in not knowing yourself. I do not intend to sound crass, but to not know oneself is often referred to as ignorance. In this case, ignorance is not bliss. Just because a person does not take the time to learn about themself does not mean there is nothing to worry about. In fact, the opposite is true because it will be difficult to lead self or others with insight. The discipline of self-leadership is a direct reflection of your ability to lead others. It is that simple.

People are more apt to follow a leader who walks the walk rather than simply talk the talk. There are many examples of leaders who tell followers to do something or not to do something, but their actions are totally opposite. I venture to bet several names came to mind as you read the statement. Integrity is indispensable. Misalignment of words and behavior leads to a question of trust.

Trust is essential in establishing a solid core to develop yourself as a leader. Being believable is key. Though not perfect, President Barack Obama comes to mind when I think of decency and believability. He presents himself as a positive and effective leader. As indicated by many political polls, he is well liked and well respected by most. The President appears to be dignified and treats others with kindness. He is a loving husband to his wife, displaying outward signs of affection. He is a great father, as his children were well mannered and polite while in the White House. Again, he is a good example of credible leadership. In today's political and social climates credibility does not seem to matter. However, I refuse to allow those who feel as if they can deceive others and not be held accountable, or at least be called out on their lie, to be the norm.

We all face challenges and setbacks. And though this idea is not new, you are in control of how you handle those challenges and setbacks. We all have a story. But here is the beauty about stories, they can be rewritten, and endings can change as long as we hold the pen. Your life path is all about you. It is about your mindset, your choices, and actions. Andy Andrews, author of *The Traveler's Gift: Seven Decisions that Determine Personal Success*, notably said, *"First we make choices. Then choices make us."* What do you want? I was confronted with this question as I sat on the ledge of that windowsill at the age of 14 and have been confronted many times since.

What do you want? It's all about and up to you.

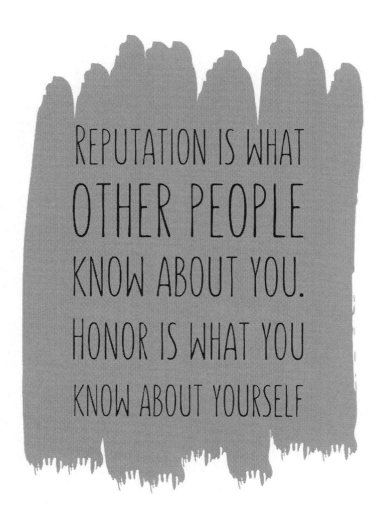

REPUTATION IS WHAT OTHER PEOPLE KNOW ABOUT YOU. HONOR IS WHAT YOU KNOW ABOUT YOURSELF

Breathe deep. Inhale and exhale slowly three times.
Ponder this question...Who are you?

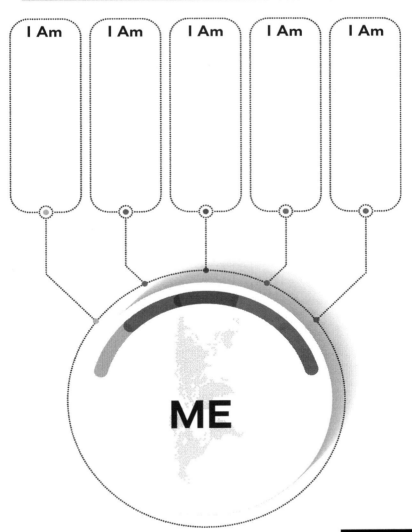

I don't cover my face because I want to show my identity.

-Malala Yousafzai,
Pakistani activist

What can you do to promote yourself to the next big role or status in your dream self?

It's All About YOU

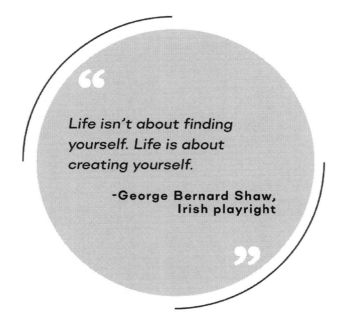

> *Life isn't about finding yourself. Life is about creating yourself.*
>
> **-George Bernard Shaw,**
> **Irish playright**

It's All About YOU

Chapter Two

POUR ON THE PASSION

PASSION

"AN INTENSE DESIRE OR ENTHUSIASM FOR SOMETHING."

According to a recent job satisfaction survey, only 20 percent of those surveyed reported having a passion for what they do. That leaves a whopping 80 percent of surveyed population reporting they are either unhappy or unsatisfied with the work they do. For the 80 percent, I wonder how much effort or level of excellence is considered when performing jobs where passion is absent. The negative impact must be noticed at some point.

Passion is defined as "*a strong liking for or devotion to some activity, object or concept, a deep interest.*" I have often asked myself—how do I find passion? What is my passion? When asked, world-renowned motivational speaker, Dr. Kimbro would respond, "Whatever it is you enjoy doing, and you would do it for free, that's your passion." My initial response was, "Huh!" Then I thought about it. I thought of all the successful people who started out doing what they do for little or no money. When I think of Dr. Martin Luther King Jr., Nelson Mandela, Rosa Parks, and many others, I think "They could not have been in it for the money."

While others may suggest what you are good at doing or what lights your fire, no one can define your passion. For me, passion is about the things I love to do. I know I am passionate about something when it commands my attention. I think about it continually and it is difficult to get thoughts of the idea out of my head. Sometimes I scribble notes or will talk out loud about what is constantly on my mind. And, if you are anything like me, when you are in the midst of doing something that brings you pure joy or in a conversation about something that you are passionate about, you might lose sense of awareness. Generally, passion is something we cannot ignore.

In all His infinite wisdom, God blessed each of us with special gifts. What are you good at doing but does not take much effort? When you identify that thing and develop it, grow it, I believe you discover the essence of gift. Notice I said to identify (take note), develop (perfect it), and grow (share with others). Just because you are good at something it does not suggest you do not have to develop the gift. Often development leads to growth.

When thinking about gifts and passions it is important to note a distinction. A gift is something you do. Passion is how you feel about what you do. Comedian and TV Personality, Steve Harvey, would suggest you "Pour your efforts into your gift, not your passion." In other words, ignite passion for your gift. This idea was further floated during an interview I conducted with Dr. Dennis Kimbro. He stands by the notion that *"A passionate committed mind cannot be defeated. A burning desire, that inner flame cannot be extin-*

guished, but you have to act on it." Action is required. You must do something with your gift for it to flourish and become passion.

One of my favorite quotes is by Henry David Thoreau, an American author.

"Don't die with your music left in you."

Though the death of Kobi Bryant, superstar basketball athlete, was tragic and shocking, I smile when I think of him and this quote. He sparkled as an example of someone who poured passion into their gift. I did not know Kobe personally; however, I could feel the passion he had for the game of basketball and winning. During an interview I recall how he expressed the desire for greatness in his craft or gift. As a result, he won five NBA Championships. And if that was not enough, he created a documentary about his love for the game that earned him an Oscar Award. He remained focused and poured everything he had into his gift. That's passion. Kobi's passion was so noticed that it was only after retirement from the game that others noticed his intensity levels lowered. Stephen A. Smith, Journalist for ESPN said, *"Kobe is the happiest I've ever seen him in his life. He's laughing, cracking jokes, and loving on his family. He's a different Kobe."*

It is not too late to discover your gifts if you are still alive. This means God has a purpose for you. No matter how old or young you are, find a passion that fuels your gift. I want to give honor to a man whose passion for years served him well. He helped others to transcend his level of personal commitment. Colossians 3:23 reads, "And whatsoever you do, do it heartily as to the Lord and not unto man." Dr. Martin Luther King, Jr. understood his work. His passion was driven by his love for the Lord. He wanted to give to God as His Son gave to us.

Another great man that comes to mind is Nelson Mandela. A South African antiapartheid revolutionary political leader and philanthropist, he was the country's first Black head of state and the first elected in a fully representative democratic election. Mandela spent 27 years in prison fighting for others and the injustices enacted on them. Passion according to Dr. Kimbro, "is like a burning desire, an inner candle—a flame that cannot be extinguished." For 27 years and until his death, Mandela still had a flame burning inside of him.

Dr. Martin King Jr., and Nelson Mandela used their passions to motor their gifts. What are your gifts? What do you pour your passion into? No matter how young or old you are, you have a gift or gifts that can be developed with purpose. Fuel your gifts with passion and watch how they grow to spread impact and influence others.

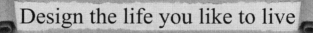

Design the life you like to live

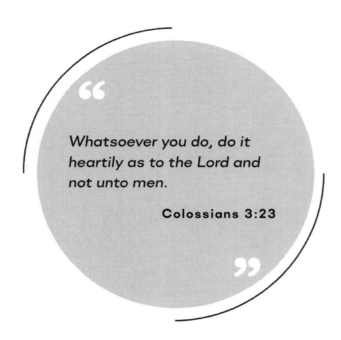

"

Whatsoever you do, do it heartily as to the Lord and not unto men.

Colossians 3:23

"

It's All About YOU

ACTION PLANNING
Note a few of your most important goals. Identify the plan for achieving the goal, action steps, and timeline for completion.

GOAL	PLAN	ACTION	TIMELINE

GOAL	PLAN	ACTION	TIMELINE

It's All About YOU

> **"** The more time you spend contemplating what you should have done...you lose valuable time planning what you can and will do.
>
> **Lil Wayne,**
> **Hip Hop artist**
> **"**

Bucket List:

1.

2.

3.

4.

5.

6.

It's All About YOU

7.

8.

9.

10.

11.

12.

13.

14.

15.

> **"**
>
> *Without leaps of imagination or dreaming, we lose the excitement of possibilities. Dreaming, after all, is a form of planning.*
>
> **Gloria Steinem,**
> **American journalist**
>
> **"**

It's All About YOU

Chapter Three

FACE YOUR FEARS

FEAR

"AN UNPLEASANT EMOTION CAUSED BY THE
BELIEF THAT SOMEONE OR SOMETHING
IS DANGEROUS, LIKELY TO CAUSE PAIN,
OR A THREAT."

When I was 13, I wanted to be a lifeguard at the local Boys and Girls Club. I passed every physical test that was required of me, but there was one test I feared. I feared it because it required me to tread water in the middle of the deep end of the pool.

Bozeman, the lifeguard instructor, was a big, tall man. He created an obstacle course in the pool that required each swimmer to push past him and swim through various large rings. During the course another person or two would swim out of nowhere to try and divert your attention from the large ring. Each swimmer had to aggressively break past the obstacles and successfully maneuver through the rings. Before my turn in the water, I saw several guys defeated by Bozeman. They would dive into the water with confidence and slowly rise out of the water deflated. Just watching this scenario play out repeatedly was enough to shut me down. And apparently, I was not the only one intimidated. Several of the guys waiting their turn in line eventually walked away before they made it to the front of the line. I must admit, fear had set in, and it felt as if my knees were knocking. I was about 5' 1", 125 and no muscles for years to come. There was no way I was going up against this grown man. Fear was slowly smothering my dream of becoming a lifeguard that summer.

As I waited my turn, a memory flooded my mind. I remembered when I was nine years old, my

It's All About YOU

father took my brother and I to the beach for the first time in our lives. He wanted to be sure we knew how to swim, or at least scrap enough to save ourselves if in a large body of water. When he told us to walk out in the ocean until the water covered our heads, we screamed and hollered, "Like little girls", so he said. We embarrassed and disappointed our father terribly. He took us home and whooped our butts. And that was not the end of it. He told us we were going back the next day and he would spank us again if we acted like screaming nuts. My brother Glen immediately conceded and told dad he was not getting in that big bathtub.

The next day we went back to the beach. The fear of spanking and disappointing my father was far greater than the fear I had of the water. Remembering that day at the beach and many times more, I faced Bozeman and successfully completed the lifeguard test course. I worked as a lifeguard for the Henry Horner Boys and Girls Club several years and trained others throughout that time.

When I look back over my life, there are several times when I gave fear too much power. I now realize the opposite to be true. Fear can empower me and you as well. Think about it. Whenever you have conquered something you feared, you probably became even more emboldened. Conquering fear has a way of empowering. So, instead of shying away from things or circumstances I fear, I now ask "What am I really afraid of, and what is the worst that can happen?". When I identify the source of my fears, I can more appropriately deal with whatever is causing the hesitancy. Likewise, I can rationally think about the worst-case scenarios and how I can deal with those as well if they should come to fruition. This thought process empowers me because my thinking or belief system generally shifts for the better.

This is not only true for me but for you as well. Think about watching a baby take his or her first steps. That first step led to many falls, getting up, falling, and finally led to running. Suddenly the world seemed to open and new life was discovered. New challenges were presented and somehow that child who some time ago took a first step is now treading new territory.

It takes faith, belief in oneself to step into the unseen. Alexi Panos and Preston Smiles, authors of *Now or Never: Your Epic Life in Five Steps* suggest often fear is trying to tell us one of two things — either a breakthrough is right around the corner or run like hell because whatever it is may not be good for you.

The first was true for me as I thought about writing this book. I certainly had fears. Not only am I not a good writer, I had fears around whether anyone would buy the book, or at least read it if I gave it away. Some of that fear still exists but I refuse to be crippled by it. Through life experiences I have learned that no matter how perfect you think you are, or something is, someone will find a flaw. So be it.

Whether it is writing a book, relocating to an unfamiliar place, starting a business, public speaking, or simply introducing yourself to someone new, fears can be conquered. Sir Edmund Hillary, the first man to climb Mount Everest, proved this point. The takeaway is that he did not allow fear or the thought of failure to discourage him. His courageous feat furthered inspired others to take on the challenge. And he was inspired to do even more.

What would you risk overcoming your fears? Will you risk your reputation? What about your finances? Would you risk failure itself? Several years back I was confronted with these questions. I had dreams of starting a talk show after watching many episodes of the Arsenio Hall Show. So, I funded my own show with hopes of picking up sponsors to cover the tri-state areas of Indiana, Michigan, and Kentucky on the local cable channel. To pitch the idea, I had to executive produce the show myself. I included my sister as the entertainment—world class jazz vocalist and a local celebrity in Chicago. As the host of the Latham Live Show, I shot a 30-minute segment and ran it through a 60-day subscription I purchased to the local cable channel. My hope was to pick up sponsors. A lot of people viewed the segment, and I got a great deal of feedback. Unfortunately, I ran out of money to invest and did not secure sponsors to continue funding. I was one and done, but I did it.

Okay, I know this question is overused but it is a critical one. What would you do if fear were not a factor? I mean seriously. What would you attempt to do if you knew there was no way you would fail? Would you train for a marathon? Venture out in a start-up business? Design a clothing line? What would you do? What would you dare to dream if fear did not flood your emotions? I love how Dr. Howard says it— *"F.E.A.R. is the Front Entry to A-new Reality"*. In other words, fear is the gap preceding a new reality or experience. What will you give to experience something new, exciting, life-giving?

feel the fear
and
do it anyway

Facing Fears

What I Notice About Myself When I Feel Fear?	What I Can Do to Better Cope?

It's All About YOU

> *The brave man is not he who does not feel afraid, but he who conquers that fear.*
>
> **Nelson Mandela,**
> **Former President of South Africa**

Think of someone you admire. How do they show courage in the face of fear? How can you demonstrate those qualities in your own life?

It's All About YOU

One of the greatest discoveries a man makes, one of his great surprises, is to find he can do what he was afraid he couldn't do.

**Henry Ford,
American industrialist**

It's All About YOU

Chapter Four

CREATE THE CHANGE YOU WANT

CHANGE

"MAKE OR BECOME DIFFERENT; TAKE OR USE
ANOTHER INSTEAD OF."

I am writing this chapter at the beginning of a nationwide quarantine in the United States of America. The world has been attacked by a sinister and deadly virus that has created havoc on the entire world. Our government leaders and scientists are scrambling to contain the virus and to come up with an antibody that can stop and protect millions of people from dying or contracting this deadly disease. At the time of this writing 83,424 people have lost their lives. First responders, doctors, nurses, and other medical personnel are among the dead. It is a dark, depressing, and dangerous time.

By the time you hold this book in your hands, hopefully our nation, the world is past this nightmare. But here is the deal—each of us gets to decide if we are going to allow the madness to consume us, or if we are going to pivot. Linda Clemons, a Body Language Expert, and great friend of mine, would say this means we have to change the way we look at and manage calamity around us. You know this but let me remind you—you can only control you. You can change the way you think about a situation and suddenly the situation seems to change.

If you fix your mind on negativity or confusion, you become part of the problem and progression ceases. Valuable time is wasted, and productivity may appear out of reach. I think this is a good place to insert

a reference to one of my favorite scriptures when dis-
cussing change and challenges, 2 Corinthians 4: 8-9.

*We are hard pressed on every side, but not
crushed; perplexed, but not in despair; persecuted, but not abandoned; struck down,
but not destroyed.*

Currently we are in bleak times. For many,
it may appear as if there is no purpose to life or that
troubles are too much to handle. I do not believe there
is anywhere in the world where the virus has not
impacted human life. However, faith in God and in
humanity will not allow us to succumb to the troubles.
Now, and in all times of trouble, consider how you look
at problems. Again, to quote Dr. Howard, "How you see
what you see, determines what you see." How you see
darkness determines what you see in the dark. How
you see light determines what you see in the light.

There are times when you may be perplexed, but as the scripture suggests, do not be in
despair. Life happens and there will be times when
you are persecuted or cast down, however you are not
abandoned or destroyed. A virus can come in many
different forms—job loss, failed relationship, financial

devastation, or perhaps a serious health issue. Whatever the form, according to 2 Corinthians 4: 8-9, you
are not forsaken.

I invite you to consider or change your perspective about any form of virus. Trouble may be on
every side, yet do not be distressed as you travel life's
journey. Admittedly, I too was tested when I realized
the impact of Covid-19 to my employment and life-
style. My initial thought was how am I going to fulfill
my financial obligations if I am not working? I was not
only concerned and nervous, but straight up panicked.

However, I have never been one to hold on
to negative thoughts for too long. I woke up the next
morning after my last day of work and decided to go
for a workout. I put on my running shoes, workout
gear, and drove to the parking lot of my home church,
Eastern Star Church. I parked the car and after sitting
for a few moments, I proceeded to walk around the
church. The longer I walked, the more peace poured
over me. Three and half miles later, my mind and my
body were at total peace. I had prayed and mapped out
a plan for survival.

A confused mind would have difficulty coming to a place of peace during what seemed like chaos.
Without a doubt, I experienced a mind changing
moment as I walked around my Father's house and

looked up at the cross. Every time I lapped the building, I thanked God for grace and mercy. As I sat in the car before heading home, I was reminded of Dr. Willie Jolley, a motivational speaker, and his take on dealing with change, or a new normal. He shared many great nuggets and I would like to share a few of them with you here.

1. Remain calm. When you are calm you can think more clearly.

2. Do not choke. Choke is another word for panic.

3. Do not stop breathing. Pay close attention to your breathing pattern. Be sure to inhale and exhale deeply several times throughout the day.

4. Do not stop living. Life happens and whatever happens, keep moving.

5. Do not participate. Be mindful of the news you consume and how you respond.

Here is the truth. How you view problems affect your spirit and your outcomes. How you look at life can stop or start what you pursue. I will add a number 6 to Dr. Jolly's list—do not stop thinking about the power. That is the power of God that is within you. Dr. Jolly would advise you to pray and then move your feet.

According to the Good Book, *prayer without works is dead.*

You can see your problems but fix your sights on the goal. Life passes more quickly than most would like. Instead of waiting for your ship to come in, swim to the ship. Changing how you think is a powerful tool. Your thoughts can sink you or propel you. You get to choose. Change your mind and your mind will change you.

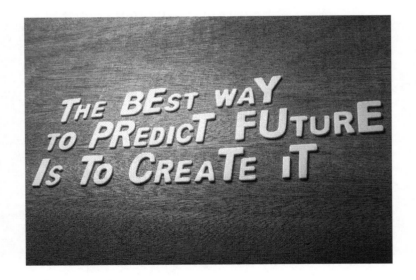

It's All About YOU

People can cry much easier than they can change.

James Baldwin,
American novelist

Think about a change you would like to make (life change, behavior change, career, etc.). Map the steps you will need to take to make it happen.

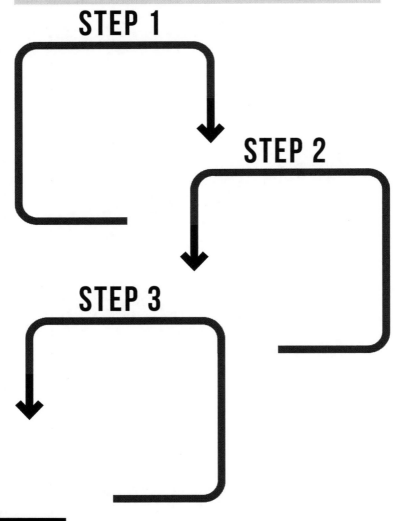

STEP 1

STEP 2

STEP 3

It's All About YOU

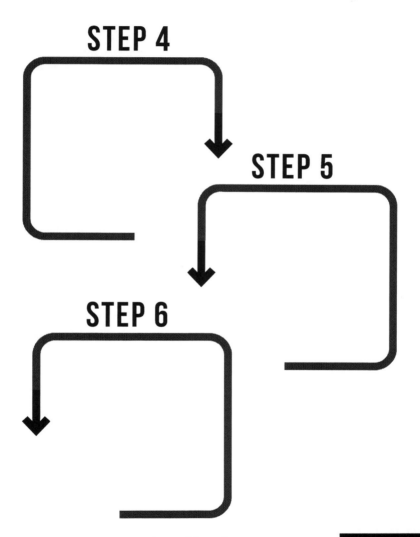

STEP 4

STEP 5

STEP 6

Identify a past failure or something you wish you would have done differently. What changes would you make? What are the most valuable lessons you learned?

It's All About YOU

> *The world as we have created it is a process of our thinking. It cannot be changed without changing our thinking.*
>
> **Albert Einstein**
> **theoretical physicist**

Chapter Five

KILLING TIME
KILLS TIME

KILLING TIME

"TO DO SOMETHING THAT IS NOT VERY INTERESTING OR IMPORTANT TO PASS TIME."

I must submit. I am guilty of one of the most unforgivable offenses known to man—in my opinion. I stand accused of killing time, or procrastination. Writing this book is a 12-year project. I wrote parts of it that remained in my computer for 12 years. Yes, 12 years. It was not until I attended a conference and met my current book coach that I started to think differently about what I wanted to write and whether I could even complete the project.

I was intrigued after hearing Dr. Howard's presentation on *How to Write a Book in 31 Days*. I told her that I had started writing a book 10 years ago, but it was still on my computer. She was nice about it, but with a slight smirk and high-pitched voice said, "You need to publish it." Three months later I saw her again. She asked if I had made any progress with my book. I just smiled. This time she was not having it. "I'm not fooling with you" she smiled. That day those words did something to me. I knew she was not being cruel, but the words were like a jolt in my chest because I knew I was procrastinating. I said to myself, "The next time I see her, I'm going to hand her a manuscript." Another three months and I saw her again. I did not say a word, but simply handed her my manuscript. She took it and said she would give me feedback.

As I reflected on the length of time I sat on this project, I was embarrassed. For so long my go-to lines where *I'll finish*, or *I'll start tomorrow*. But my tomorrow was pushed further and further down the road. In my mind I would think, *I got time*. This became my excuse repeatedly, until it became a habit to respond with one of those phrases. How many times have you been guilty of killing time, or procrastinating? How many times have you been guilty of doing everything but doing nothing? Killing time is a time killer—if you get my drift.

Procrastination is defined as *the action of delaying or postponing something*. This is intentional and requires action. If you are guilty of procrastination, you are guilty of making conscious efforts or decisions. Procrastination indicates a decision to put off. By putting off, you decide to do something else instead. While there may be times this is not as costly to you in accomplishing a goal, there are times when the investment is astronomical. Sometimes waiting can allow you time to get a better perspective and sometimes it can cost you missed opportunities. The point is this, when you make a habit of procrastination, you risk productivity. Too, research shows that people who procrastinate experience frustration, guilt, stress, and anxiety more so than people who do not procrastinate. In some cases, procrastination has been known to lead to serious issues like low self-esteem and depression. I can certainly attest to the poor self-image, as I mentioned feeling embarrassed about procrastinating when writing this book.

I know so many people who have a tendency of putting off decisions or goals they want to accomplish. Some people are good at putting life decisions away in a box with good intentions of getting to them one day. Well, the road to hell is paved with good intentions. I have heard *"I'm gonna"*, *"I was getting ready to"*, or *"I'm going to start next week"* too many times to count. You have probably heard them too, or even said them yourself. If you are careful, procrastination can become the norm, or a way of doing life.

I came across an article in *Psychology Today* that identified drivers of procrastination from factors such as low self-confidence to anxiety, a lack of structure, or an inability to motivate oneself to complete unpleasant tasks. Research has also shown that procrastination is intricately linked to fixation on negative thoughts.

Though there are many ways one might suggest overcoming procrastination, Les Brown, a world premier motivational speaker, targets focus as a plausible cure. During an interview Brown said, *"One of the key things you have to have in order to become successful is focus."* Focus steers you to stay the course and accomplish what it is you want to do, even when distractions sway. Brown proclaims procrastination can be addressed with clear focus and determination.

Imagine waking up on any given day not knowing it is your last. I believe you must live life with some sense of urgency. If starting a new company is what you want to do, do it. If you want to shed a few pounds, stay focused and do it. Whatever it is you have not started because you lost focus, reimagine yourself accomplishing your goals.

A year from now you'll wish you had started today.

	Sun	Mon	Tue	Wed	Thur	Fri	Sat
12 am							
1 am							
2 am							
3 am							
4 am							
5 am							

	Sun	Mon	Tue	Wed	Thur	Fri	Sat
6 am							
7 am							
8 am							
9 am							
10 am							
11 am							

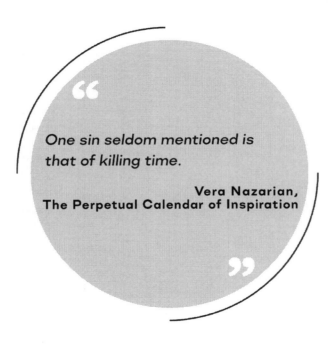

One sin seldom mentioned is that of killing time.

Vera Nazarian,
The Perpetual Calendar of Inspiration

It's All About YOU

What observations do you notice when reviewing your Week Log?

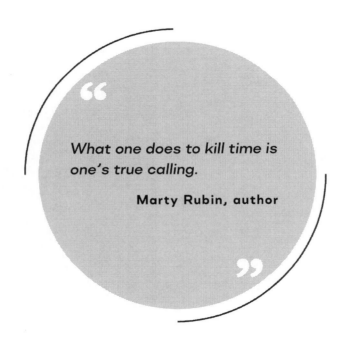

> *What one does to kill time is one's true calling.*
>
> **Marty Rubin, author**

It's All About YOU

Replace the idea of killing time. Think about something you have been procrastinating to do. Decide to create a new habit for attaining what you want. Track your consistency for one month.

HABITS TRACKER

HABITS

○	○	○	○	○	○	○	○
○	○	○	○	○	○	○	○
○	○	○	○	○	○	○	○
○	○	○	○	○	○	○	○
○	○	○	○	○	○	○	○
○	○	○	○	○	○	○	○
○	○	○	○	○	○	○	○
○	○	○	○	○	○	○	○
○	○	○	○	○	○	○	○
○	○	○	○	○	○	○	○
○	○	○	○	○	○	○	○

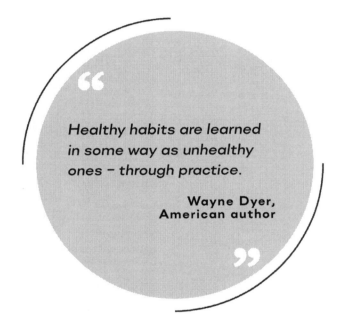

Healthy habits are learned in some way as unhealthy ones – through practice.

**Wayne Dyer,
American author**

Chapter Six

EMBRACE ADVERSITY

ADVERSITY

"DIFFICULTIES; MISFORTUNE."

Does adversity have value? This is an interesting question because on the surface adversity and value are oxymorons. Most people avoid adversity at all costs. However, the value of adversity is immeasurable. Often adversity renders growth in relationships, finances, or perhaps in emotional wellbeing. And inevitably, growth is imminent, whether in a positive direction or in a negative direction. Nothing remains the same, including reluctant humans.

The notion of change even through reluctance became clear to me amid adversity. My ex-wife and I were forced to file bankruptcy. At the time, I thought bankruptcy was equivalent to financial failure. Not to mention the embarrassment and humiliation. As I sat in the dark basement of our home I was flooded with shame. I need to figure out what to do next.

I got involved in real estate in the early 2000s. The business was booming, and I saw boundless opportunities to cash in on the market. I was ambitious and knew real estate investments were a sure way to establish sustainable wealth. It did not take long for me to acquire 18 rental properties across the city. Business was going well. I quickly rented property as single family dwellings and started to see clear returns on my investment. Well, until the real estate market crashed right before my eyes. Renters were not consistent with payments, and I was not able to repay what I had borrowed from the bank. Just as fast as I had rocketed to success, I plunged in defeat. I quickly sold off some of the properties but could not recover what I owed. Realizing I was in deep, I filed for bankruptcy on 1.3 million dollars to save as many of my personal gains as possible.

Filing bankruptcy was one of the most difficult decisions I have had to make to date. I was humiliated, frustrated, and felt an immediate sense of failure. Looking back, bankruptcy seemed like the only plausible way to get out from under the pressure of default on many levels. It felt as if I had defaulted not only in my finances, but personally as well. And though I was surrounded by chaos, I was blessed at the same time because I did not have to give up the home I had at the time. And even more importantly, my marriage sustained throughout the adversity.

Though I would have preferred not to experience what I went through in losing the rental properties and filing for bankruptcy, I can honestly say good did come from the ordeal. Even though it was a difficult time, it allowed me to reflect and learn to put fearful encounters in God's hands. Afterall, I still had my health, strength, and a positive mindset. I continued to work in the hair care profession as a stylist and eventually worked my way out of that mess. I did not give up on dreaming scary goals or taking risks.

Though on my back, I could look up and get up from that crippling situation. The bottom line is this, I realized I was not built to stay down. So, I continued to move and to make things happen as best I could, given the circumstances.

No matter what I go through or what adversity I face, I know I can rise above it because I have done it before. Both success and failure leave clues. When you go through something traumatic and blessed enough to rebound, you know God will not let you down in the future. It was during that time, I knew if, and when faced with adversity in the future, I would be able to handle it and overcome it.

Learning that lesson has served me well. It began to shape me earlier in life, though I was not quite attuned to the messages. When I heard about the all-male high school on the South side of Chicago, I was admittedly curious. From what I had been told, the school was like no other education experience I had encountered. The school produced a lot of notable athletes, and the active academic program was well known as notable and distinguished. Hales Franciscan High School had a reputation as one of the best schools for developing young men into college material. Coming from the ghetto, this was an attraction for my mom in making the decision to send me there.

Talk about adversity. I had to be out of bed and dressed by 5:30 every morning to get breakfast before catching the train to transport me across town. Five days this was the routine. I went back and forth. I was up early and returned home late into the evening. To add to the challenge, I had to navigate gangs on the street to get back to my home safely. I had many run-ins and faced much ridicule because I attended an all-male Catholic high school. The fellas on the streets felt some kind of bad way about me appearing to be different—or thinking I was better than them. This was their sentiment not mine.

Anyway, my mom and dad finally understood my frustration with getting up early and getting home late. The routine had taken a toll on my academic progress. So, I moved in with my dad and stepmom, Floydie, who lived on the south side of Chicago. A year later, my youngest sister, Kelly Rose was born. She was named after Aunt Rosie, my dad's oldest sister. Kelly graduated from Northeastern University and is a proud veteran of the U.S. Navy. Thank you, Sis, for your service.

Living with my dad, I could now get to school 45 minutes earlier. With this, I was able to participate in sports after school. I began to thrive at that school. Eventually I graduated from Hales and was accepted at Loyola University of Chicago where I received a B.S. degree in criminal justice.

Again, though I was presented with many challenges at Hales Franciscan High School, I realized how a change in environment can affect your capacity to achieve. I know the trajectory of my life was changed in large part to the change in environment. I formed several long-lasting relationships at Hales—two specifically. Alvin "Butch" Taylor and Gary Kimbrough became two of my best confidants. Butch and I lived on the South Side of Chicago and rode the bus to school together. This gave us a lot of time to get to know one another and discover that we shared similar experiences in growing up in the projects. I connected with Gary as a teammate on the basketball roster and grew to appreciate his friendship. Your circle of influence matters.

There were days when I had to physically fight, mentally fight, and fight academically. But the mere opportunities to fight have played a huge role in who I am today. The experiences related to Hales Franciscan High School taught me valuable lessons I have shared with others over the years. Without a shadow of a doubt, I know where you come from does not necessarily determine who you are. You can become prey to a negative environment, or you can prowl around, over, or into the circumstances to become better.

Adversity can be viewed as an opportunity to add versatility (flexibility and resources) to your repertoire. If you can embrace adversity and expand creativity, resilience, and perspective, you will be, do, and have that which you may have imagined possible. Strap on adversity as a weapon, part of your arsenal if you will, to become the best version of who you were created to be in the universe.

What I Learned in Adversity

There are thousands of self-help books and coaching programs that deal with the topic of adversity. The information highway is flooded with insight on how to overcome foreseen and unseen mishaps or troubles. In the next few minutes, I want to share what I learned in facing adversity. No matter the circumstance, big or small, I have learned to deal with adversity in the same way.

1. Before and above anything, I learned to pray faithfully. This may not be news or new to you, but it became crystal clear for me in one of my most vulnerable moments. If I was going to get up and get out of the situation I was in, I had to

believe in something, someone much bigger and more powerful than I was at the time. I needed the strength of someone else. I had friends who intervened and offered to help me, but it was not enough. Call it male ego but I was too full of pride to ask for what I needed anyway. I appreciate the help my in-laws at the time offered, but still this was not enough. I needed a higher source, The Source. The only way to tap into the strength I needed was through prayer.

2. What I know for sure if you need a plan of both action and activity. Action is simply making a move to do something. Activity is being consistent in whatever actions you take. If you act but not carry through in activity, you'll likely make little progress. Change is seen in creating a plan of action and working the plan consistently until you see the results you desire or until your soul is satisfied in peace.

3. Keep pushing. The initial plan you set out on a journey with may not work. Your plan must be exhaustive. This means you have a plan and plan to back the plan in the event something goes awry in the first plan. In other words, you must have the mindset that failure is not an option—it only serves as information on how to keep pushing. Giving up is not part of the plan. It cannot be a talking point.

It's All About YOU

Problems are not
stop signs, they
are guidelines

What action(s) can you take in the next 30 days that will move you closer to your desired outcomes in the following areas?

Relationships:

It's All About YOU

Spiritual Health:

Physical/Mental Health:

It's All About YOU

Finances:

> *You may encounter many defeats, but you must not be defeated. In fact, it may be necessary to encounter the defeats so you can know who you are, what you can rise from, and how you can still come out of it.*
>
> **Maya Angelou, activist, and novelist**

It's All About YOU

Describe a time when something unexpected happened or was thrown your way. How did you adjust at that moment? What did you learn from the experience that you can apply to future situations that require flexibility?

It's All About YOU

Success is to be measured not so much by the position that one has reached in life as by the obstacles which he has overcome.

**Booker T. Washington,
American educator**

It's All About YOU

Chapter Seven

MAKE MOTIVATION A CLOSE FRIEND

MOTIVATION

"THE GENERAL DESIRE OR WILLINGNESS OF SOMEONE TO DO SOMETHING."

When I entered Loyola University of Chicago in 1978, the school was 98% White. Coming from an all-Black boys' catholic high school, this was a culture shock. I had never been in the presence of so many people who did not look like me. This was a challenge unlike others I had before. I was challenged at almost every level of my existence at the time. It started with my belief system. I thought White folks were naturally smarter. It was an idea planted through my childhood interaction with society. I had been conditioned and the conditioning was working. I entered Loyola University as an intimidated freshman and early experiences continued to affirm stereotypes I had encountered.

I can recall an incident that happened early on in my college career. At the end of class my English professor asked that I see him after class. Once all the students exited, I went up to the front of the classroom.

"How did you get into this school?"

I was shocked. "What do you mean? I asked.

He repeated, "How did you get into this school?"

By now I am almost speechless. "What do you mean? How do you think I got here? I guess my SAT scores and high school grades got me here."

What he said next became a turning point for me. In that moment something switched, and I knew I had to dig deep, but had to prove a point.

"I don't think you have what it takes to finish school here. You are not equipped to be here." He said, looking me straight in my eyes. He did not flinch or hesitate.

For a lack of being able to come up with anything better in the moment I responded, "Well, that's your opinion but thank you."

All I could think was he just gave me the fire I need to finish and finish strong. I got up from the desk where I was sitting, walked out of the door, and walked directly to the registration office to drop that course. There was no way I was going to pass that course. The professor has perceived ideas about who I was as a person and student. As far as I was concerned, I was doomed from the start and could not see the situation getting any better.

Though I was mad and disappointed in that English professor, I was also armed with everything I needed to meet the challenges I would face for the next four years. And boy would I need fire power?

It was not shortly after the meeting with the English professor that I was summoned to the office of history professor. Earlier in the day he had returned a graded assignment. I looked around the room and it appeared everyone had their paper back with a grade on it except for me. The professor stood in front of the room and held my paper in his hand. It had to be my paper because I was the only student who had not gotten an assignment back.

"Mr. Alexander, I need to see you after class in my office."

Nervously I said, "Okay."

Class resumed and I tried as hard as I could to concentrate. It was difficult because as you could imagine, I thought about all the possible scenarios he could have wanted to talk to me about related to that paper. Was it that bad or that good? What the heck could he possibly have to say that needed to be said face-to-face?

After class I waited around a few minutes and proceeded to his office.

"Who wrote this paper?", he asked as he tapped the paper against the palm of his hand.

"Excuse me", I asked as I shifted the weight from one side of my body to the other.

Then he asked even more directly, "Did you write this paper?"

I said, "Yes I did."

And as if I were not honest, he said "I'm going to need you to bring in all the materials, the research you used to my office tomorrow. I don't believe you wrote this paper."

"I told you I wrote the paper", I said.

He repeated, "I don't believe you wrote the paper so bring me the research."

The next day I took all the materials I had gathered in writing the paper to the professor's office. Without saying a word to him, I sat everything on his desk as he sat close by in his chair. Just as I entered, I left his office. I did not say a word.

Before class started the next day, the professor walked over to my desk and handed me my graded assignment. I opened the folded pages and saw an A circled on the page. Though I stewed a little, I was relieved at the same time. At the risk of appearing arrogant, after class I approached the history professor.

"I don't know how you are a professor at this school. You questioned my work because I am Black. My high school prepared me well."

That was the only incident I had with that professor. I decided I was not running away from another challenge at Loyola. Four years later at graduation, the English professor was the first faculty member in line as I walked past and received my diploma.

There are several other stories from my college and since that have influenced or motivated me to specific action. Sometimes motivation comes from some type of external influence and sometimes you may be compelled by intrinsic promptings. Whether extrinsic or intrinsic, your attitude, or how you view the push is what makes the biggest difference.

The basis of motivation is to have a motive to do something. This is a reason that may or may not be obvious. This is not a new idea. You have likely heard that determining your WHY is critical to maintaining motivation. This is important because WHY you do something generally drives HOW you do it. Les Brown, motivational speaker, would say, "When your WHY is big enough, you'll find the HOW." As you hold motivation close like a friend, you are in tune to yourself and your rationale for different behaviors. In other words, you become more intentional and self-aware.

In the larger sphere, you are more vigilant and vision oriented. Motivation is bigger than a feeling or the energy to accomplish a task. It is a north star, a guide that navigates your direction.

Motivation has served as a north star in many of my encounters. When I was six years into my career as a stylist and working as a technical educator, I had a clash with motivation. The job required that I fly all over the United States and abroad to teach salon owners how to run a more profitable business with products. I did not own a salon at the time but had a lot of practical experience as a business owner. A close friend, Charlene Carroll, pulled me to the side one day. The short of the long is that she suggested I needed to open a salon of my own. Well, I was not hearing it at first. I had heard all the nightmare stories about maintaining the flow of the business, employees, payroll, and on and on. I did not want that headache, though I was teaching salon owners how to run their own businesses. Huh!

Charlene eventually convinced me that I needed a salon to increase my credibility as an educator of business owners. She thought it was rather odd of me to be telling business owners to do something I had not done myself. And she was right. Her motivation, or rationale, motivated me to open a salon. My salon became one of the best known in the city and top in commissions earned. I had control of the daily operation and the opportunity increased my credibility as a platform artist and business owner at the same time. My confidence increased as a teacher to other entrepreneurs. I elevated my presentations and was able to use more relevant and personal illustrations while sharing my story. I could legitimately tell salon owners and those who wanted to get in the business, how to operate as a solopreneur. As a result, I generated personal business and expanded my experiences and interaction in the salon world. Ultimately, I learned how to start a product line of my own.

My journey to own a salon was sparked by the motivation of a friend, Charlene, and blossomed into a full-service salon. Without that initial encouragement, I do not know if I would be where I am now in business. Charlene is a legend in the salon business and because she believed in me, I believed in myself. Her and her husband Ron, a decorated retired Boston firefighter, have been in my support corner for years. Here is the real deal, you need people in your corner who authentically want you to be the best version of yourself.

The word motivation suggests movement or motion. You may be able to start initiatives yourself. Others of you may need a little push. Either way, when someone you respect believes in you and raises you up to higher levels, you are apt to strive even further.

Thank God I had people like Charlene, Ron, and my cousin, Glenn Alexander, who got me into the business around me to see for me what I could not see for myself. They held a space for me until I could fill it with my own belief. Take a moment and think about your motivators. Who are the people you can count on the most to motivate you to become your best?

Motivation has a way of stirring something within you that you may not be aware you even had. When I reflect on those early days in my business, I am proud. My name was on the front of a building on a major street in Indianapolis. To this day there are people who still talk about the happenings at Alexander's Salon. Several stylists who came through the tutelage of Alexander's went on to successful salon ownership, all because I was motivated by the motivation of others.

Whether you are motivated by positive influences like Charlene, or negative influences like several of my college professors, know that you have what it takes to make things happen as you desire them to be. Water the seeds of inspiration and support you have gathered throughout the years. Despite what anyone else tells you, you can make it happen. Allow the motivation, or motives of others to spark a fire within you.

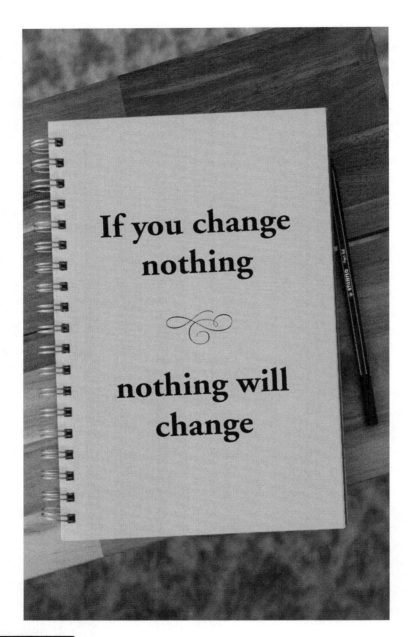

If you change
nothing

nothing will
change

What have you been talking about doing but have yet to do? Identify what is holding you back. Make a plan to "Just Do It".

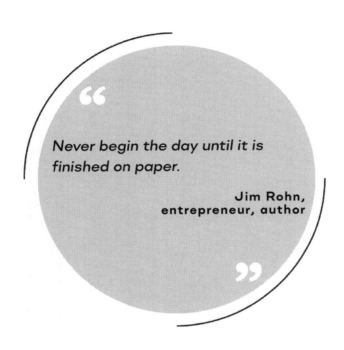

Never begin the day until it is finished on paper.

Jim Rohn,
entrepreneur, author

It's All About YOU

10 THINGS THAT
REQUIRE ZERO TALENT

BEING ON TIME

WORK ETHIC

EFFORT

BODY LANGUAGE

ENERGY

ATTITUDE

PASSION

BEING COACHABLE

DOING EXTRA

BEING PREPARED

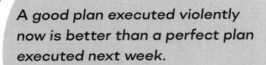

> *A good plan executed violently now is better than a perfect plan executed next week.*
>
> **George S. Patton,**
> **former Officer in the U.S. Army**

Chapter Eight

NOW WHAT?

It's About You is designed for you to ponder how you respond to and show up in the world. As Alex Preston, an American author would say, "There is a lot of information in books, but if you don't use it, it's just information." Hopefully, this book hinted at a piece of information or two you can use. Information becomes wisdom when it is used. How can you use what you have read to inspire making a difference?

Dr. Howard mentions it is selfish to be selfless. In Western civilization we are taught that we need other people. Absolutely, we need other people. However, it is also true that you need you. The Bible tells us to love God and to love people as we love ourselves. How do you love other people as you love yourself if you don't love yourself? In other words, you can only give what you got. If you only love yourself superficially, that translates to loving other people the same. So, it is selfish to be selfless. Not to focus on yourself, but rather so you can give the best of who you are to other people.

It's All About You! is not about being selfish in the negative connotation. This is about loving yourself enough to do what is best for you. It is in this space that you will relate to others in the healthiest of ways. Based on mindset, how you experience the world, and your ability to succeed constantly changes. Focusing on yourself increases your self-image and leads to self-empowerment. You can change what is possible for you by changing what you think and what you envision. My hope is that something within these pages has sparked your thoughts. The sooner the idea that It Is All You! resonates throughout your entire being, the sooner you will expand your potential to experience your best life yet.

1 year =
365 Possibilities

It's All About YOU

ACKNOWLEDGMENTS

I met many challenges through the years in thinking about writing this book. I would start, stop, start, stop, and start again. For a long time, I put the idea away and stepped away. However, I am grateful for so many people who have encouraged me over the years. Before I go, I want to specifically acknowledge a few individuals who have been particularly instrumental in getting me on the path to finishing something I started.

My children are a constant inspiration to my will for reinventing myself. I love each of you dearly — Julien Lamax, Latham Keir, Blake Raphael, Blaine Peyton, and Chase Earl. To their mothers — thank you for the gifts you gave to me.

Deagria Level, thank you for sparking a flicker to a pilot that was burning with a little hope of ever completing this work. As an author yourself, you inspire me. You are the ultimate motivator and touched me beyond what you will ever know. I appreciate your friendship, the many conversations about God, and your perspectives on life, love, and self-belief.

Linda Clemons, internationally recognized body language expert and one of the country's most prolific motivational speakers, thank you with all my heart. You are truly a gift. Thank you for sharing your vision, which I know is inspired by God. Your words of wisdom have a profound effect on my life and direction.

Pastor Jeffrey Allen Johnson, senior pastor at Eastern Star Church, under the influence of God you have fed me and thousands of others with the knowledge and understanding of Jesus Christ. Thank you for cleverly extracting messages from Scripture and applying them to our daily lives. God is essential in my life, and I have been blessed to witness many miracles He has performed for me and through me.

Phillip Armstrong and I met more than 35 years ago when I was going into my junior year at Loyola University of Chicago. Phil, you have always been strong, smart, and wise beyond your years. We connected as brothers and have since shared many thought-provoking conversations. Thank you for your positive energy and unwavering encouragement. You motivate me to be better. Thank you, my friend.

The key to helping me put this book together is my book coach, Dr. Larthenia Howard. Thank you for sharing your gift of organization, creativity, and insights. With your guidance I was able to move from blank pages and structure something that had been a long-time dream. Thank you for your patience.

> **"** *Some people say I have an attitude—maybe I do... but I think you have to. You have to believe in yourself when no one else does—that makes you a winner right there.* **"**
>
> **Venus Williams,**
> **American tennis champion**

It's All About YOU

Made in the USA
Monee, IL
27 September 2021